NoLex
6/12

PEACHTREE CITY
PLAN TO STAY™

Justin Bieber

ABDO
Publishing Company

Big Buddy BOOKS
Buddy Bios

by Sarah Tieck

VISIT US AT
www.abdopublishing.com

Published by ABDO Publishing Company, 8000 West 78th Street, Edina, Minnesota 55439.

Copyright © 2011 by Abdo Consulting Group, Inc. International copyrights reserved in all countries. No part of this book may be reproduced in any form without written permission from the publisher. Big Buddy Books™ is a trademark and logo of ABDO Publishing Company.

Printed in the United States of America, North Mankato, Minnesota.
052010
032011
PRINTED ON RECYCLED PAPER

Coordinating Series Editor: Rochelle Baltzer
Contributing Editors: Heidi M.D. Elston, Megan M. Gunderson, BreAnn Rumsch, Marcia Zappa
Graphic Design: Maria Hosley
Cover Photograph: *AP Photo*: Brad Barkett/Picture Group via AP Images.
Interior Photographs/Illustrations: *AP Photo*: AP Photo (p. 25), Scott Gries/Picture Group via AP Images (p. 11), Manny Hernandez/Picture Group via AP Images (pp. 11, 29); *Getty Images*: Craig Barritt (p. 17), Bryan Bedder (pp. 14, 19, 22, 25), Larry Busacca/Getty Images for NARAS (p. 7), © Christopher Lane/Contour by Getty Images (p. 27), Frank Micelotta (p. 13), Christopher Peterson/BuzzFoto/FilmMagic (p. 9), Craig Sjodin/Disney Channel via Getty Images (p. 21), SEBASTIAN WILLNOW/AFP (p. 5).

Library of Congress Cataloging-in-Publication Data

Tieck, Sarah, 1976-
  Justin Bieber : singing sensation / Sarah Tieck.
    p. cm. -- (Big buddy biographies)
  ISBN 978-1-61613-974-2
  1. Bieber, Justin, 1994---Juvenile literature. 2. Singers--Canada--Biography--Juvenile literature. I. Title.
  ML3930.B416T54 2011
  782.42164092--dc22
  [B]
                         2010013413

Contents

Justin's first album is called *My World*.

Music Star

Justin Bieber is a talented singer. He is best known for singing popular music. His albums and songs are well liked around the world.

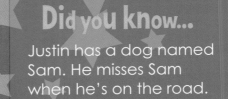
Family Ties

Justin Drew Bieber was born in Stratford, Ontario, Canada, on March 1, 1994. Justin's parents are Jeremy Bieber and Pattie Mallette.

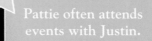
Pattie often attends events with Justin.

CANADA

Ontario

Quebec

LAKE SUPERIOR

Michigan

LAKE HURON

Stratford

LAKE ONTARIO

LAKE MICHIGAN

LAKE ERIE

New York

UNITED STATES

Ohio

Pennsylvania

N
W · E
S

Justin's parents separated when he was young. His mother raised him in Stratford. There, Justin attended school and was a good student.

Growing up, Justin did not see his dad very often. Yet, they grew closer over the years.

Justin got all As in school! He enjoys writing.

Did you know...

Justin wrote the song "Where Are You Now" about missing his dad.

9

Starting Out

From a young age, Justin was a talented singer. When he was 12, he entered a local singing contest. He earned second place!

Family and friends wanted to see Justin perform. So in 2007, he and his mom began to post videos on a Web site called YouTube. That way, people could watch him sing.

Justin has always loved music. He took drum lessons. And, he taught himself to play the piano, the guitar, and the trumpet.

Big Break

Millions of people saw Justin perform on YouTube. One of them was a music **executive** named Scooter Braun.

Scooter saw that Justin had talent. So, he brought Justin and his mom to Atlanta, Georgia, for a meeting. Scooter wanted to help Justin record an album. In 2008, Justin signed a record deal. Scooter became his **manager**.

Did you know...

Famous singer Justin Timberlake also wanted to work with Justin. But, Justin decided to work with Usher instead.

Scooter introduced Justin to famous singer Usher (*right*). Usher helped Justin record music.

Justin and Usher became friends.
They have recorded music together.

Soon, Justin and his mom moved to Atlanta. There, Justin was closer to his work. He began to record songs for his first album. Justin sang pop and rhythm and blues songs. He also worked with private teachers to keep up with school.

First Album

Justin enjoys making music videos. He is a skilled dancer.

Justin worked hard to record songs and videos for his album. He **released** four songs before the album came out. These singles were "One Time," "One Less Lonely Girl," "Love Me," and "Favorite Girl."

Fans became very excited about the songs. They were hits before Justin's album even came out! This rarely happens for new artists.

Justin travels around the world to perform.

Did you know...

Justin has performed for the U.S. president! He said it was exciting to meet Barack Obama and his family.

In November 2009, Justin **released** his first album. It is called *My World*. It sold many copies during its first week. Within two months, it went platinum. This means it sold more than 1 million copies!

A Singer's Life

As a singer, Justin spends time practicing his songs. He works with people in the music business to improve his sound. They often work together in recording studios, where albums are made.

Justin has been a guest on television shows and radio stations, such as Radio Disney.

Did you know...

Justin often wears a dog tag necklace. This was a gift from a fan.

Did you know...

Justin has appeared on the
Nickelodeon show *True Jackson, VP*.

Singers also spend time **promoting** their music. They may travel for several months on a concert tour.

After his first album came out, Justin worked hard to promote it. He appeared on television. And, he performed live for fans.

Fan Fever

Over the years, many music artists have become very popular. Some couldn't even walk down the street because fans got so excited! These include Elvis Presley, the Beatles, the Jackson Five, and New Kids on the Block.

Like these performers, Justin has very excited fans. One time, more than 3,000 fans came to a shopping mall to meet him!

Many people want to meet
Justin and see him perform.

John Lennon, Ringo Starr, Paul McCartney,
and George Harrison were in the Beatles
(*above*). Beatles fans (*left*) were so excited to
meet them, police had to keep control.

Off the Stage

When Justin is not working, he spends time with his family and friends. He likes to dance and go out on dates. And, he has fun making jokes. Justin also enjoys spending time online.

Sometimes Justin sends messages to his fans online. He uses the Web sites Twitter and YouTube.

Did you know...

One of Justin's favorite colors is purple. He often wears colorful sneakers. He especially likes high-tops.

Justin is very well known. Reporters often take his picture. And, fans ask for his autograph.

Buzz

In March 2010, *My World 2.0* was **released**. This is the second part of Justin's first album. That summer, Justin had his own concert tour.

Justin's fame continues to grow. Fans are excited to see what's next for Justin Bieber! Many believe he has a bright **future**.

Snapshot

★**Name**: Justin Drew Bieber

★**Birthday**: March 1, 1994

★**Birthplace**: Stratford, Ontario, Canada

★**Albums**: *My World, My World 2.0*

Important Words

executive a high-level employee who manages or directs a company.

future (FYOO-chuhr) a time that has not yet occurred.

manager someone who directs the work of a person or a group.

promote to help something become known.

release to make available to the public.

rhythm (RIH-thuhm) **and blues** a form of popular music that features a strong beat. It is inspired by jazz, gospel, and blues styles.

Web Sites

To learn more about Justin Bieber, visit ABDO Publishing Company online. Web sites about Justin Bieber are featured on our Book Links page. These links are routinely monitored and updated to provide the most current information available.

www.abdopublishing.com

Index